"Ever wonder why Paul s̶ ̶ ̶ ̶ ̶ ̶ ̶ ̶ ̶ ̶ ̶ ̶ ̶ ̶ these is love?' Ed Gross personally and pastorally reveals the simplicity and complexity of love. Read his words, listen to his heart, and you will find yourself drawn to a deeper love for Jesus Christ and for other people. This is a book to move your heart, so be prepared to change and to love it."

> Dr. William Krewson
> Chair, Undergraduate School
> of Bible and Ministry
> Philadelphia Biblical
> University

"This is a helpful book, wise and spiritually alive, intended for use in personal devotions or small group studies, and reminding us of the love of God as the great theme that stands at the very core of Christian faith and life."

> Dr. Gary D. Badcock
> Peache Professor of Divinity
> Huron University College
> London, England

"This in depth, biblical study of the love of God will not only broaden your knowledge of this wonderful subject, but will challenge you to look honestly at your own practice of true biblical love. Read it carefully, especially with a desire to apply its teaching to your own life, including your relationship with God and with others."

> Dr. George Murray
> Chancellor, Columbia
> International University

"Ed Gross is a thoughtful pastor and a good scholar. But this little book doesn't come from Ed's head, it comes from his heart; and to read it properly you need to open your heart and let it be bathed in the love of God. Ed himself will tell you that there is nothing new in what he writes–but it is a message we need to hear over and over, and it was a joy and encouragement to let Ed's passion touch my soul deeply."

Rev. Stephen Smallman
Director, Birthline Ministries

"Agape love demands that we step outside of our comfort zones and be willing to sacrifice for those who often spit at us in return. It is the love modeled by Christ on the cross, when he said, 'Forgive them, Father....' It is impossible for us to give this kind of love unless we have first experienced such a love from God. Sadly, we as the church often do a poor job in modeling that which we have received in abundance. Pastor Gross, though, reminds us that once we *have* experienced this kind of love from Christ, it *ought* to be impossible for us not to share such love with others."

Pastor Win Groseclose
Westminster Presbyterian
Church
Rocky Bayou Christian School

"The first epistle of John states - herein is love, not that we love God, but that he first loved us.... This reality allows for us to approach Christ's summary of the Decalogue - love God and love our neighbor, with intentionality. Ed Gross helps us understand these truths in very practical ways using a simple, non-technical language in doing so. I would recommend this book to all generations."

Pastor Zachary Ritvalsky
Sweet Union Baptist Church

"As a local church pastor, it is my supreme task to assure parishioners are on a spiritual growth track that leads to ... spiritual maturity in Christ. Such I believe is accomplished through multiple ministry mediums, even guest pastors ... invited to minister in my local church context .... At a Sunday morning worship service ...Pastor Ed Gross spoke ... on the topic of 'Let Love Win Through You.' The message's content and delivery, most certainly propelled by God's Spirit, created a spiritually attentive and sobering atmosphere that obviously resonated with the hearts of congregants and even inspired a post-message response of many who acknowledged an immediate need for transformation in their love relating to God, oneself or others. The challenge of the message resoundingly reminds Christians in any church or ministry context of the chief priority of loving God and others 'purely' and therefore 'triumphantly' in the whole of their living and service for Christ. Apart from such our pursuit and practice of Christian love is lost at the heart level."

"'Let Love Win through You' is destined to be one of God's tools of the twenty-first century which universally sharpens Christians' perspective and practice ... of Agape, providing elements of healing and health to hearts and lives in need of God's renewing love."

Pastor Ronald Parks
Philadelphia Bible Fellowship
Community

As Ron has just testified, Ed loves to preach and teach on the theme of Christ's love. He is available to speak for you in Sunday sermons, Saturday workshops or weekend conferences/retreats. Contact him through his website: www.edwardngross.com

Let
Love
Win

Through
YOU

ED GROSS

Let Love Win Through YOU

© 2010, Ed Gross

ISBN: 978-0-557-31914-5

Cover Photo:
© Gino Santa Maria - Fotolia.com

Makarios Publishing
Fides Quaerens Intellectum

Published by Lulu.com

$\mathbb{I}$ dedicate this book to my beloved mother, Ruth Sligh Gross, whose love of Christ, fervent prayers, thirst for Scripture and zealous example have helped shape my life since that night long ago when we both came to faith in Christ in Greene, NY.

viii

Preface

We are all facing a serious problem. A problem so menacing that it threatens everything in our lives. This danger takes many different forms. We see it in Christian men wrestling with either passivity or pornography. Or when Christian women are fueled with anger or fear. It may be the cause of Christian kids letting go of their faith. Or in pastors losing heart. It threatens singles embracing hopelessness or depression. And seniors who wonder what they have to live for. In the Church as many of us know it, there seems to be a general powerlessness. A lack of enduring joy. An unsettling worldliness. Little longing for prayer. Very few who seem to be walking with Jesus. What is the problem?

The Bible reveals that there is one big cause for all of these and many other struggles. It is this— our leaving the love of God. So this little book aims at defining, describing and dealing with that sin. And calling us all back TOGETHER to Jesus. To his life of love.

The love-problem is everywhere. So, when I am asked to speak to a church or a class. If I were to sit down with you. Whenever I have just one shot. Or one series of messages. The message in this book is what I say each time. It is that important. That fundamental to everything else. Miss this and nothing makes sense. Nothing works. Everything falls apart – just as God said it would.

This message is on my heart because it has always been on God's heart. I am his child. I have given my heart to be re-formed by him. And this is what he is doing. He is re-creating me, his son, in his image of love. Slowly but surely. And if you are his child, you are my spiritual sibling. A sister who has surrendered your will to Jesus. A brother in whom the Father is working. He is doing the same great thing in us all. Pouring his Spirit of love deeply into the shafts of our souls. If we are open to it. If we remain thirsty for the living water. As our wonderfully changed brother Paul wrote, "…God has poured out his love into our hearts by the Holy Spirit, whom he has given us."[1]

If you have not yet dared to trust God with your life, you may find yourself wanting to do just that as you read further. This type of love is what you have always wanted for yourself. And true, unfailing, eternal love is exactly what you know everyone else is longing for.

I am writing this book at this time because my sweetheart, my wife Debby, said I should. And that means a lot to me. She has been by my side and seen what God has done. In me. In her. In our marriage. In my ministry. And she wants that for everyone. Love is a wonderful, living power that works everywhere. Let the love of Christ win through you.

Ed Gross – Dec 2009

---

1   Romans 5:5

Let Love Win through YOU!

Since God is Love

(Part One)

1

"*The love of God should occupy no one place in a theological system, but every place.... To write on the love of God is the Christian theologian's supreme privilege and supreme responsibility.*"[1]

"*I have written almost fifty books, and everything in every one of them might be mistaken, but this one thing has to be true: that God is love.*"[2]

1   Kevin Vanhoozer in *Nothing Greater Nothing Better: Theological Essays on the Love of God,(Wm B Eerdmans Publishing Co.)* p 29.
2   Peter Kreeft in *The God Who Loves You,* (Ignatius Press) p 12.

Chapter 1 – Since **God**

Do not let the brevity of this book underwhelm you. It is purposely short. Remember, it is really an expanded sermon. I am not writing for this to be the last word on love. It is just an important start. I hope for other books to follow that will wrestle with the many questions concerning the mystery of God's love. But now I just want to highlight its indispensable nature for you. That is all you need for now. You are likely much closer to winning in life than you think. As you read and sincerely respond to this message, you will sense the Spirit of God renewing your life with the power of Christ's love.

The foundation of God's love is absolutely safe and sure. When established, love allows the massive building called "the Christian life" or "the transforming power of the gospel in culture" to be built. To grow up strong and stable. Able to stand against any storm or war that opposes us. Our lives and witness, without this foundation of love, will collapse.

Each of the first three parts of the book is devoted to one of these clear foundational principles. Part One: God is love. Part Two: Love mattered most to Jesus, to Paul and to the local church. Part Three: Love never fails. Given these three truths, love can win through YOU! And that is Part Four.

Everything of importance starts with God. He is the One who is infinitely greater than everyone and everything else. We get our life from him because he is the Author of life. Life in its entirety, therefore, is his gift to us. So every moment and every living person we enjoy or disdain are part of his plan. God is before, in and after it all. He is there. And he always matters most.

God should be our main thought. Not the moment we are in. Or the object we are observing. Every thought in life should find room for God, the Life-giver. The Bible begins with God. "In the beginning God...."[1] In all the debates that follow, we should never forget this fact. Before any physical thing existed, God was alive. He is primary. We are not. The main thought always to have is simply "God is in this now." So, when Moses wanted a name that would shock the Israelites to the core. A name that would end all discussion and get them moving. God told him, "This is what you are to say to the Israelites, 'I AM has sent me to you.'"[2]

This little book is about winning in life. Rather than losing. In every area of life. In everything. And right here at the beginning you must grasp this one thing. Winning is a gift from God. Experiencing joy rather than sorrow depends chiefly on him. Not on you. Not on your tenacity or spirit or resources. Everything begins and ends with Jesus. He said, "apart from me you can do nothing."[3]

If you awoke this morning and your first thought was not of God, you awoke foolishly. You started off unwisely. The psalmist long ago wrote, "In his pride the wicked does not seek him; in all his thoughts there is no room for God."[4] Before you think this refers to others, let me simply ask you, How many of YOUR thoughts center on God? If you are like me, you will answer, NOT ENOUGH. Perhaps even, NOT MANY. And maybe, ALMOST NONE. But don't get too upset. Remember this isn't chiefly about you or me. It is about

---

1   Genesis 1:1
2   Exodus 3:14
3   John 15:5b
4   Psalm 10:4

4

God. And that is very good news. He loves us even when we forget him. "The Lord knows the thoughts of man; he knows that they are futile."[5] Nevertheless he loves us.

Love leads us away from ourselves. Self-focus leads to futility. Self-absorption is dangerous. It yanks the world out of its amazing God-created orbit and tries to force it to revolve around US. Too many times a day we slip into this selfish madness. That is why Jesus came. To save us from our sin. From our self-centered insanity. To bring us into the blessedness of a God-centered love. So we can really see. Really live.

Don't waste your energy by trying to corral all of your wildly straying thoughts. You are not strong enough. Too many Christians try that route. We think too highly of our own strength! Self-discipline is not the **key** here. Yes it is part of it. But not the main part. The key is love. Discipline flows from love. It only trickles from everything else. Do you have a difficult task to get done? Give it to someone who will love doing it. Love creates discipline.

The reason we Christians do not think more on God is that we don't take the time to develop love for him. We love ourselves and our things more than we love God. So, as we begin, remember--our need is not chiefly for greater resolve or commitment or focus. It is for greater love. Most of us need to love God far more than we do.

So start with that. Asking God to fill you with love. With his love. And ask him to do the same for everyone who picks up this book. And for everyone you know. And you will be well on your way to letting love win through you.

---

5   Psalm 94:11

For Reflection or Discussion:

How often each day do you think about God?

At what point and for what reason do these thoughts usually start?

"The love of God. We have lost it today; we have turned our back on the ocean and are looking over barren, colorless hills for the ocean's fullness…. Drink deep and full of the love of God and you will not demand the impossible from earth's loves; then the love of wife and child, of husband and friend, will grow holier and healthier and simpler and grander."[6]

"The God-relationship is the mark whereby love towards men is recognized as genuine love. As soon as a love-relationship does not lead me to God, and as soon as I in a love-relationship do not lead another person to God, this love, even if it were the most blissful and joyous attachment, even if it were the highest good in the lover's earthly life, nevertheless is not true love."[7]

6   Oswald Chambers in *The Love of God (Discovery House Publishers)*, p 17.

7   Soren Kierkegaard in *Works of Love(Harper & Row Publishers)*, p 124.

Chapter 2 – Since God *is*

God is not only the first or most important Being. He is also near. "Not far from each one of us."[8] Giving us all "life and breath and everything else."[9] Yet not crowding us. Or pushing us aside. Think of it. We like to be in the center of pictures. That's where they put the important people. Right in the middle. You are in the center of God's picture. And he is there with you, with his loving arm around you. For all to see. When was the last time you proudly showed that picture to someone? Or talked about Jesus as your dearest Friend? Have you forgotten that amazing fact?

How *real* is Jesus to you? Do you think of him as *really* dying for you? As actually risen from the dead with you? As never leaving or forsaking you? You can't think of him in those ways without genuine faith. Without trusting in someone you cannot see.

We don't think about Jesus at those times when we do not need him. When all we need is ourselves. When we can really exist by our own wits or by our own efforts. Then, in those thoughts, we do not make room for Jesus. Because we do not sense that we need him at that moment. In those moments we forget that we are just creatures. And live as though we were the Creator. We forget that God **is** the One that matters. And that – we are **not**.

John heard Jesus emphasize this many times. He said such things as "I am the bread of life. I am the way. I am the true vine. I am the door. I am the good shepherd. I am the resurrection and the life."[10]

---

8   Acts 17:27b
9   Acts 17:25b
10   John 6:35; 14:6; 15:1; 10:9; 10:11; 11:25

We most often think of ourselves as providing for and feeding ourselves. As being able to figure out the best path to take. And as supporting and helping others. Rather than of Jesus as our bread, our way, our vine. We try to master the art of self-defense or get foolproof insurance policies instead of seeing God as our Good Shepherd. We sing songs like, "I will survive!" instead of trusting him every moment as our resurrection and life.

We Christians do not often view ourselves as rejecters of Jesus. But we are not far different actually from those he shocked when he said, "I tell you the truth, before Abraham was born, I am!" At that point "they picked up stones to stone him."[11] Just whom did he think he was? Obviously, he was claiming to be God. Are we all that different?

We can't stone him because he is not present with us physically. But we can resist him. Replace him with ourselves. Forget that he alone is the great **I Am**. However hard we try to be God to ourselves and to others—we fail. He alone is, "I am." We must realize, "I am not." I am not strong enough. I am not wise enough. I am not in control. I am not central. He is.

Scripture teaches that what God is, he always is. He is unchangeable in his essence. Not more or less from one moment to the next. Eternally the same. "God is not a man, that he should lie, nor a son of man that he should change his mind. Does he speak and then not act? Does he promise and not fulfill?"[12]

You can't escape him. He is *really* all he has claimed to be. Make sure you grasp this truth and never let go of it: **God is!** Paul put it like this, "Let

---

11   John 8:58,59a
12   Numbers 23:19

God be true, and every man a liar."[13] Many are near to remind us during those times when God appears to have withdrawn from us and seems not to be actively helping us or our cause. We are counseled that we better take matters into our own hands and not be too spiritual. Don't believe them. God is enough! You are not.

There is a reason he appears sometimes to be disconnected from you and your problems. There is a reason he cannot help you at times. And that is not because he lacks either the power or the desire to help us. The reason rests with the nature of true love. He doesn't intervene sometimes because his love forbids it. Once you grasp this, when you understand the unchanging nature of his love, your life will change forever. You will begin to appreciate both the priceless worth and the tremendous power of that love. You will clearly see why Satan's ceaseless strategy has always been to divert Christians from letting Christ's love win through us.

For Reflection or Discussion:

How desperately do you really need Jesus?

In what ways do you naturally meet your own or others needs without dependence on him?

---

13   Romans 3:4b

"And so it is that with love, we are at the center of everything in the teaching of Jesus… When taken together with such Johannine statements as ' God is love' and 'God so loved the world' such texts (as Mk 12:28-31) rightly lead us to conclude that we have in the concept of love a kind of symbol of the whole of the Christian message, both in its foundations in the being and acts of God and in its application in the spiritual life. Theologically, everything is to be located and found here; everything is to be organically developed in relation to this one concrete concept."[14]

"This statement, "God is love," is so profound that no less than Augustine saw it as an important evidence for the doctrine of the Trinity. If God is love—that is, if love is intrinsic to His very nature—then he has always loved, even from eternity past, before there was any created object for His love….Clearly the love this text describes is an eternal reality. It flows from the very nature of God and is not a response to anything outside the person of God. The apostle does not say, 'God is loving,' as if he were speaking of one of many divine attributes, but 'God is love'—as if to say that love pervades and influences all His attributes."[15]

---

14   Gary Badcock in *Nothing Greater Nothing Better,* p 30.
15   John MacArthur in *The Love of God (Word Publishing),* p 29.

Chapter 3 - Since God is *love*

$\mathcal{A}$re you now confused, wondering, "How can the love of God prevent him from rescuing us or answering our prayers?" That makes no sense to many of us. Because love, as we know it, doesn't behave that way. We would definitely respond to those we love by helping them as quickly as we could.

The problem is that we do not really know love in its purest form. Scripture says, "God is love." We are not love. We have fallen away from him and from his love. We do not innately understand love. But God does because he is love. All he does and does not do shows love. He defines what love should and should not do because he is love. All the time.

Apply this to Jesus. Everything he did and said was love. John wrote, "This is how we know what love is: Jesus Christ laid down his life for us."[16] We do not know love in its perfect form (agape) except through Jesus. Paul Miller depicts Jesus correctly in his wonderful book about Jesus entitled, "Love Walked Among Us." Even when Jesus did not run to heal Lazarus, but waited. As amazing as it seems, that was motivated by love. Or when he refused to talk to the Greeks who were seeking him. That refusal was based on love. How would your love have responded in the following story?

"As Jesus was getting into the boat, the man who had been demon-possessed begged to go with him. Jesus did not let him, but said, "Go home to your family and tell them how much the Lord has done for you, and how he had mercy on you."[17] Does that look

---

16   1 John 3:16a
17   Mark 5:18-19

and sound like love to you? The poor guy just wanted to be near him. To learn and grow. Jesus said, No. And that was love because all Jesus did and did not do was love.

God's love is perfect love. Our love is imperfect. Incomplete. We have many loves that are lower and lesser than the complete love of Christ. Our lesser loves are dim reflections of his full, brilliant agape-love. Problems arise when we grab hold of one of our lesser loves and make it our definition of love. Mistakenly making a small love into true, perfect love. Like when we call kindness, love, as we often do. When we refuse to see that there are times when love MUST look and feel unkind. When love demands pain.

When a child needs an injection and looks at you with tears and pain wondering WHY would you let the doctor hurt him with that sharp needle. Or when disease invades the body, love demands that pain be experienced. It never seems kind when we allow or prescribe a painful remedy. But that does not make it unloving. True love is more than merely seeking the comfort of another. Love seeks the good of the other. And what is good for another is not always accomplished by their being free of pain. Kindness then, though an important part of love, is not love in its fullness.

In a larger book we could see this is true of everything we call love. Each aspect is only a small part of love. Consider erotic pleasure. The joy involved in sexual intimacy is often a wonderful experience. There is often great joy in that type of love. But that is not all that love is. When a person or a culture (like ours) calls having sex- "making love"- they are bound for great disappointment. Because love is much bigger and more wonderfully fulfilling than just sex. But make no mistake, the God who made us male and female, created us for sexual pleasure in the context of marriage. He is delighted whenever we both, male and female, are delighted and fulfilled by it. But love continues when sex ends.

What is it to love? *True love selflessly seeks the good of one's beloved.* True love flows outward. It is "never self-seeking."[18] Never absorbed in itself. Self-focused. Our lesser love of self-love is automatically selfish. It is good to have self-respect and a positive self-image. But that lesser love must be enhanced with many other types of love. Or it becomes ugly. We all naturally seek our own good before the good of others. We abuse the proper limits of self-love and want to use others for our own pleasure or profit. All such inward focus falls short of God's glory. Of his perfect love. So, we can conclude that selfish love can never lead to lasting happiness. Never.

Another aspect of love is what I will simply call a typical mother's love. A bend-but-won't break love. If this was the only type of love you have experienced at home, then you were certainly blessed with love. It was the amazing love of a mother. A patient, persistent and forgiving love. But, like all loves below God's agape love, it is a lesser love. Not love in its fullest and finest form. Because love sometimes does what a typical mother cannot instinctively do. Agape will let its beloved one go. God's love is freeing. A love that does not seek or demand control.

An aspect of perfect love is that it will not force itself on the beloved. Against the will of the cherished one. God's love nurtures freedom. So, he allows a Christian to follow his own carnal desire because that is what his heart wants at that time. And that always

---

18   1 Corinthians 13:5b

leads into trials and pain. We lead ourselves away from God, loving someone or something else more. Until that pursuit fails and we return in repentance back to our first love. Until we give God our whole heart. Our full love.

Satan kills and destroys. He oppresses, intimidates and enslaves. Satan's love is totally selfish. It is like rape. Rape is a perversion of self-love. In rape, a man brutally uses a woman as an object to meet his own sexual desires. He stalks and forces and threatens and defiles. He overpowers the will of his victim. But God doesn't rape us. He loves us. He leaves the Christian free to decide whether he wants to love God or not. True love will let the beloved walk away. Rather than forcing him or her to stay against their will.[19]

Some of the trials that come into our lives are on account of our lack of love. We all-too-often replace the love of God with a lesser love. And we cling to it, madly thinking that it will satisfy us. Even though it never has and never can. We try again to get happiness from fulfilling the desires of self. We think that this time the result will be different. That our self pursuit might work. It might satisfy, leaving me better off than before. But it doesn't. It can't. Satan, the liar, is the Prince of selfishness. Jesus, the true Lover, is the Servant of all.

Love in its fullness flows from every part of a person's being. It involves mind, emotion and will. Right now we are focusing on the way that love is connected with volition. With our wills. True love involves desire and choice. We long for our loved one to freely and spontaneously express his/her love to us. Nothing makes us happier than that. Love between persons

---

19   Read Hosea

demands a free choice and not coercion.

Our triune God is three persons with one perfectly shared nature. The Father, Son and Spirit are love. As persons, they desire to be loved by the Christian. They give us a new will in spiritually birthing us. A will that can choose to love God. Every believer is re-created with a new nature of love in the new birth. This is what is called our "first love."[20]

Once our wills are renewed and true love is reborn in us, the Trinity wants us to exercise it to use and grow the new ability he has given us to love. We have seen that God's command to love him is our first and primary duty. Scripture also portrays God as desiring our love. As being ready to respond whenever love is truly motivating the believer. But waiting until love is present. Until we truly desire him. Until we choose to think and feel and act out of love for him.

This is one reason why our prayers may not be answered.[21] Or why our lives may not be rescued from trials. Because we don't always pray out of love. In fact, quite often our prayers are fueled by selfishness. And selfishness is never true love. Sometimes we ask God to help us or others out of difficulties. Rather than asking him to sanctify the trials by leading us or others through them into a deeper love. Rather than desiring to walk with God in undisturbed love, we want the trial to end because we are just tired of the hurt and the struggle. Focusing on ourselves and not him. The pain of discomfort often motivates our prayers more than the pain of not loving him. We often forget that love is the main thing. And securing it for ourselves and others is better than anything else. Better even than

---

20   Revelation 2:4 and Matthew 24:12
21   James 4:1-3

painlessness.

So, God will let us go our own way. He will let us pursue our lesser loves rather than quickly force us back. Why? Because love is both patient and kind.[22] And when we turn in love back to him, he is always like the prodigal son's father who "while he was a long way off, his father saw him and was filled with compassion for him; he ran to his son, threw his arms around him and kissed him."[23]

If we were God, we would likely force goodness to happen. That is because we do not naturally know how to love. Love always respects the other. Even to the painful point of letting the beloved make foolish choices. Like running off after other loves. Read Hosea and you will understand that God's love desires and longs for the beloved to love him back. Freely and joyfully.[24] Understand this point and you will better grasp the deepest sorrow of Jesus when he walked among us. Always loving and often unloved in return.

The way of the Holy Spirit, the Spirit of Love, is the way of peace. Not pressure. We can understand many mysteries in this life when we understand that true love can wait. Love "always hopes, always perseveres."[25] And since God is infinite love, eternal love – his waiting may take the shape of many days, months, years or centuries. He is never indifferent. Never cold. We misread him whenever we think he doesn't care. Because he is love, don't expect him to intrude where he is not lovingly invited or sincerely sought. As this settles into your heart, you will better understand both true love and the true God. And you

---

22   1 Corinhians 13:4a
23   Luke 15:20b
24   See also Genesis 3:1-9
25   1 Corinthians 13:7b

will be willing to let love win through you, no matter how long it takes. Or how many times the ones you love walk away from the love of God pouring out through you to them.

For Reflection or Discussion:

How would you define love?

Describe what love looks like in a few settings.

20

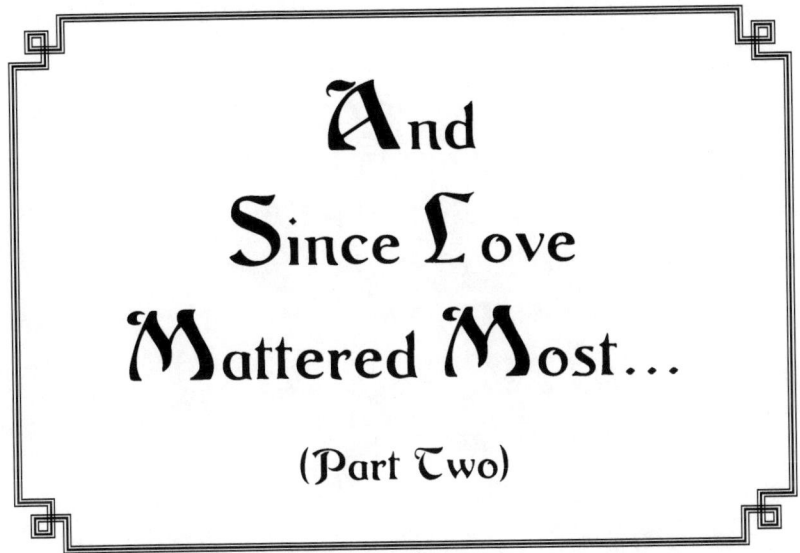

And Since Love Mattered Most...

(Part Two)

"But we should not ignore ... the danger of intellectual arrogance. Biblical scholars, theologians, and other Christian academics are easily tempted to think that they are obeying the first command simply because they work in the intellectual arena and happen to be Christians....We cannot ignore the brute fact that this first command of Jesus is not a command to think but a command to love."[26]

"So anyone who thinks he has understood the divine scriptures or any part of them, but cannot by his understanding build up this double love of God and neighbor, has not yet succeeded in understanding them."[27]

26   DA Carson in *Love in Hard Places (Crossway Books)*, p 22.
27   Augustine in *On Christian Teaching*, 1.36.40.

Chapter 4 – Since Love Mattered Most *To Jesus*

As a Christian, this chapter holds the key to changing your life and the others you would like to see transformed. In whatever ways they need to be changed. If you really get it. If you embrace this one great truth of God and do not let it go. Only if you make love first and demand everything else to take their places under it. Then your life will never be the same. And neither will the lives of those you meet.

It is this simple: Jesus taught that love was the most important thing in life. With it, the sky is the limit. Without it, you will fail. Let the following text sink into your soul and change your world. Because it will!

"One of them, an expert in the law, tested him with the question: 'Teacher, which is the greatest commandment in the law?' Jesus replied, *'Love the Lord your God with all your heart and with all your soul and with all your mind.' This is the first and greatest commandment. And the second is like it:"* 'Love your neighbor as yourself.' All the Law and the Prophets hang on these two commandments."[28]

Think of it! God was asked what mattered most to him. And he gave a clear answer. End of debate. No further questions needed. Never ever forget that, according to Jesus, love matters most to God. Does love matter most to you?

Don't answer that question too quickly or lightly. Really reflect on it at the end of this chapter. For depending on your answer, you determine how often you are standing with or against God.

Here's another question. Since love is the most

---

28   Matthew 22:35-40

important single thing, why should you ever allow it to take second place? Why should love EVER be displaced by any other thought, emotion or choice in our lives?

You see, Jesus said love should consume every thought, all of our soul and motivate every muscle in whatever we accomplish.[29] God commands it. He wants love. He demands love. All of the time. In everything.

Did Jesus say anything here that is difficult to understand? It seems rather clear. But it is obviously not easy. In fact, he said it is impossible. Thankfully, the ability comes from God. So, be encouraged "for nothing is impossible with God."[30] By God's help, you can become vessels of constant love. Not perfectly. But to such a degree that you and others will be amazed! And God will be delighted with you because you have begun to desire what he desires most.

The problems that have hindered your Christian life, have all arisen by your letting go of the love of God. Or allowing it to become second place. If your church is not flourishing and making its mark in your community, it is because somewhere along the line love was displaced by another goal. Love went out of focus. When love stays first, the God who is love is pleased. And our victorious God allows love to win through us.

Jesus demanded love to God and love to our neighbor. They go hand in hand. Two sides of the same coin. And coins minted only on one side won't buy you anything. So, love that is either only spiritual (to God) or physical (to neighbor) won't get you anywhere. Such love is a counterfeit of the true love of God. The love that filled Jesus and sent him into a world of sinful,

---

29   See also Mark 12:30
30   Luke 1:37

selfish neighbors.

Maybe you have studied the Bible for many years. Maybe not. All I can say is—your Bible interpretation and application have been truly accurate only if you have let love breathe through them. No outcome other than love is legitimate. Since God is love. And the Bible is the Word of God. So, the Bible is everywhere the Word of Love.

All the Law and the Prophets hang or depend on your handling their truths in love. All the Old Testament and subsequently, all the New Testament are only empty shells when love is omitted from them. A picture is enjoyed when it is hung on a nail that has been hammered in the wall. The nail has a very important role. Take away the nail and the picture crashes to the ground. Take away the love of God from any passage, any sermon, any application of any text—and it crashes to the ground. It becomes a mess. That's what God said about his Word.

Love with all you heart. All your soul. All your mind. All your strength. All of us. All the time. The focus has been set. Love for God and others. A selfless, other-focused love. This is what Jesus wants of you right now. In ten minutes. In ten years. In my writing this book. And in your reading it. In worship. In work. In marriage and child training. Eating. Talking. Listening. God wants us to be filled with his love. Since love matters most to Jesus. Since love filled him all the time. If you are his follower, then love will be your life.

I can assure you that if you will make the love of Christ your quest, you will soon find it. And be filled with it. Be encouraged – love can win through you!

For Reflection or Discussion:

Is the love of God the one constant force driving your life?

If not, what has taken its place?

"If any one of the fifteen attributes Paul lists (in 1 Cor 13) is to be selected as the one closest to the heart of agape, it would be that 'agape does not insist on its own way (seek its own)."[31]

"The love of God is not merely to be analyzed, understood and adopted into holistic categories of integrated theological thought. It is to be received, to be absorbed, to be felt. Meditate long and frequently on Paul's prayer in Eph 3:14-21."[32]

31   Peter Kreeft in *The God Who Loves You*, p 82.
32   DA Carson in *The Difficult Doctrine of the Love of God*(*Crossway Books*) , pp 80-81

Chapter 5 – Since Love Mattered Most *To Paul*

ℒove mattered most to Jesus. So it also should have filled those he called to follow him. You can't follow a God who is love without being a lover, too. The next two chapters show us a follower who remembered this. And a church that did not.

Paul was writing to Christians at Corinth. An amazing church, but one that was divided. With each group elevating its own favorite leaders and distancing itself in ways from their fellow Christians. This self-seeking spirit grieved Paul. Even though earlier in his own life he was proud of his own separateness. He had thought Gentiles were, "dogs!" And did all he could to remain aloof from them. Now Jesus had conquered his heart and filled it with his love. A love that does not make such ethnic distinctions. But loves all types of people. Paul was grieved that his Corinthian converts had turned against each other. And away from love. Because love turns toward the other. So what did he do?

He told the Corinthians, "Follow my example, as I follow the example of Christ."[33] And then he spoke of the powerful manifestations of the Spirit among them. The Holy Spirit was giving some of them miracle-working power. Paul had such powers, too. He excelled in gifts that they desired.[34] In miracles that they sought because of the esteem and renown they conferred. But Paul taught that these gifts of the Spirit were given to benefit the whole church.[35] Not as badges of special honor to

---

33   1 Corinthians 11:1
34   1 Corinthians 14:18
35   1 Corinthians 12:7

those possessing them. Many of the Corinthians were growing proud of their power. And growing apart from one another.

So Paul listed various offices and gifts in the church and then astounded his readers by declaring, "And now I will show you the most excellent way."[36] That is what they wanted to hear. Which is the super-gift? But he did not speak of a spiritual gift. The one thing that set one above all the others, he insisted, was love.

"Though I speak in the tongues of men and of angels, but have not love. I am only a resounding gong or a clanging cymbal. If I have the gift of prophecy and can fathom all mysteries and all knowledge, and if I have a faith that can remove mountains, but have not love, I am nothing. If I give all I possess to feed the poor and surrender my body to the flames, but have not love, I gain nothing. [37]

Take away love and everything becomes worthless. Heavenly worship, mountain-moving faith, astounding levels of philanthropy and total self-sacrifice mean "nothing" without love. So, to Paul, love obviously mattered most as well. It is more fundamental than worship and witness. Without it at the center, mercy ministry and prayer will fail. Yet, in the midst of all the books, seminars and preaching on prayer, evangelism, worship and discipleship – **where is the emphasis on the love of God?**

Christians are rightly focused on faith. Indeed - we are saved by faith! But, in fact, even when compared with faith, Paul would declare by the inspiration of God, "And now these three remain: faith, hope and love. But

---

36   1 Corinthians 12:31b
37   1 Corinthians 13:1-3

30

the greatest of these is love."[38] Is it possible that we have missed something so central, so key – that the Christianity we now possess is fundamentally flawed?

We pray for one another. For health concerns. For finances and jobs. For marriages and kids. We intercede for pastors when they preach and for our small group leaders when they lead discussion. How often do we pray for each one to be filled with the love of God? Why has it dropped down the list and gone out of sight when it mattered most to Paul? To Jesus? Until these questions are addressed and answered, love can never win through us.

For Reflection and Discussion:

Why is love more important and useful than miracles?

Why is church division so dangerous?

---

38   1 Corinthians 13:13

"*Why is the exalted Jesus so hard on [the Ephesians]? They could have been a lot worse. The answer surely lies in Jesus' own teaching…. The first and most important command is to love God with heart and soul and mind and strength; the second is to love your neighbor as yourself (Mk 12:28-34). We have already seen that failure to follow this pair of commands is implicated in every other sin we commit; worse, failure to obey the first commandment is nothing less than idolatry. God is de-godded. The forms and disciplined zeal may remain, but this church in Ephesus is in the throes of overturning the sheer centrality of God."*[39]

---

[39]   DA Carson in *Love in Hard Places*, pp 184-185.

Chapter 6 – And Since Love Matters Most *To the Local Church*

What is the strength of your church? The essence of your fellowship group? The bottom line that everyone takes away from an experience with you? Are you chiefly a teaching church? Or a singing church? Maybe a simple church? Or a sacramental and solemn church? Is your goal to be a friendly church? Or an outreaching, evangelistic church? Perhaps it is being a seeker sensitive church? A spiritually gifted church? Or a children's church? Has your mission statement chosen to focus on serving others? Giving? Going? Discipling? Preaching? Praying? Praising? Purpose Driven? Reflective? Responsive? Reaching every man, woman and child? What words matter most to you in how you describe yourself?

Maybe your chief goal is to be a Bible church? Or a Jesus church? Or a Holy Spirit church? A miracle-working church? A holy, reverent still small voice church? A debt free church? A Jesus is coming soon church? A community church? A commuter church? Caring? Contemporary? Conservative? EGens focused? A multi-cultural church? A multi-site church? A mega-church? A two or three believer house church? A family church? Or THE ancient church? Most churches choose a blend of some of these good things. Or they just do them naturally, without much strategizing. Could you pick out several that described your church?

By now I am sure you realize that WITHOUT LOVE none of these good goals will matter. In many churches, something listed above has unintentionally replaced the essential thing. The one thing needful.[40]

---

40   See Luke 10:38-42

Has this happened to your church? To YOU?

My point is - UNLESS THE LOVE OF GOD IS WHAT DRIVES EVERYTHING, YOU ARE IN GREAT SPIRITUAL DANGER. Disagreeing with me will not endanger you. But if you displace what mattered most to Jesus and to Paul, you are in trouble. Because Jesus made it loud and clear that when ANY type of church or group, of any size or status, replaces love with something else - it has gone astray. THAT church is off course and heading for disaster.

Love is irreplaceable. Because God is love. Any type of church that is filled with his love will make its mark. But even a church that is best prepared and placed, poised for growth - WITHOUT BEING FIRST FILLED WITH LOVE - will eventually lose its power. It will plateau, decline and die. The death may take awhile, depending on the size and the endowments. It may even grow because it has become the popular option. The going church. But it will start to die at its core. Even as it grows. And that death can be felt. You might even be sensing it now. Something has changed while doing the same things as before. Something has started to go wrong. Or has been wrong for a long time. Don't despair. Christ can help you.

Ephesus was a gifted church in a thriving city. It had enjoyed the ministries of Paul, Timothy and John. The church was planting other churches. It was standing head and shoulders above smaller, struggling faith communities. It seemed to have it all. But it was in danger. Deep danger. Jesus said that, with all the good going on, it had a fatal flaw! It was operating without being driven by its first love!

Listen and learn. Read it and truly repent. TODAY the renewing can begin through you.

"To the angel of the church in Ephesus write: These are the words of him who holds the seven stars in his right hand and walks among the seven golden lampstands: [2] I know your deeds, your hard work and your perseverance. I know that you cannot tolerate wicked men, that you have tested those who claim to be apostles but are not, and have found them false. [3] You have persevered and have endured hardships for my name, and have not grown weary. [4] Yet I hold this against you: You have forsaken your first love. [5] Remember the height from which you have fallen! Repent and do the things you did at first. If you do not repent, I will come to you and remove your lampstand from its place."[41]

Love is the main difference between the church today and the churches then. But even NT churches, like Ephesus, got off track. Like many of us. We have gotten more busy DOING THAN LOVING. In all our attempts to get it right. To be biblical. Or relevant. Many of us have lost our biblical core and relevance! Because love is both the most biblical and most relevant goal.

Christians - because Jesus lived and died for YOU - all you need do is repent and return! Thoughtfully analyze how much you think, feel, say and do THAT IS NOT DRIVEN BY LOVE. Every day. Take time NOW to reflect on how ungodly everything is without love. Because God is love. How unchristian a loveless thought, word or deed is. Because Christ is God. Love incarnate. And we are called to be his followers. To be filled and living out of his love.

What this demanded of me, as a Christian husband and father, was repentance. I had to change direction in my marriage. And as a pastor, missionary,

---

41   Revelation 2:1-5

church planter, soul winner, etc. What I needed was a renewal. I needed first-love again. The love that fills and delights. The love that once gave peace and joy. That made my heart light and free. I had to turn back and return to my childlike days of loving and living in Christ. Because too few of my thoughts were love. And even less of my feelings. Jesus said love was to be in "all your thoughts" and "all your heart." But love was not driving me. I judged others. I got angry. I did not listen well. I thought my way was usually in line with Scripture and others were off. My mind, instead of being filled with love to God and to others, was loveless for long stretches of the day. Focused on the here and now. On the job at hand. You see, I chose to drift from the safe harbor of God's love. No wonder that the day would sometimes become stormy and difficult. Like the Ephesians, I was leaving my first love. And I usually blamed it on the devil. Or on others.

I had to repent of my Christian life. Which many looked up to. I needed a life change. Because it wasn't very Christian. Very Christ-like. Very loving. Now you might not be as off as I was, but some of you may be close. It doesn't matter. If love is not on top--there is just one right thing to do. Choose love! Cry out to God and say you are sorry for letting go of love and grabbing on to something else. Give him your heart again. Let Jesus rule your feelings with his love. Let go of your lesser loves and ask him to fill you with his love. This is what the Spirit is waiting for. This is the chief roadblock. Do it now. And then you are ready to LET LOVE WIN THROUGH YOU!

For Reflection and Discussion:

What is your church, small group, youth group best known for?

And Since Love Never Fails
(Part Three)

"The point of 1 Corinthians 13 is that love is not our duty, it is our destiny. It is the language Jesus spoke, and we are called to speak it so that we can converse with him. It is the food they eat in God's new world and we must acquire the taste for it here and now. It is the music God has written for all his creatures to sing, and we are called to learn it and practice it now so as to be ready when the conductor brings down his baton. It is the resurrection life, and the resurrected Jesus calls us to begin living it with him and for him right now."[42]

"It is hard for us to conceive of anything that never fails. Our greatest heroes all fail at some point. Our electrical gadgets promise long life but grow dim and wear out. Our greatest champions do not win every contest. But love is a champion that boasts an unblemished record. It is undefeated in every contest. It never fails."[43]

---

42   NT Wright in *Surprised by Hope (Harper/Collins Publishers)*, p 288.

43   RC Sproul in *Loved by God (Word Publishing)*, p 204.

Chapter 7 – *Love always wins!*

When Paul said, "love never fails," he was affirming that it does not stop. It does not give up. Love perseveres and wins. Do you want to win? Then let God's love flow through you.

Winning in the Bible is often similar to winning in athletic contests. It often takes time and effort. Sometimes winning demands a long and very tedious process. With great sacrifice and hardship. Whether in a game or a series or a season, athletes do not expect instant victory. Every push-up or sprint or minute in the sauna is aimed at the final goal—winning.

The way of love in our lives is similar. It never fails. Love always pushes us toward victory. It always helps. Every thought, emotion and act of love is significant. It all counts. Love is never a waste. Even when it seems to be.

This is a great reason why we should let love always be the motivation for all we do. God eventually will win. God is love. So the way of love will eventually win.

This will appeal to some of you more than others. If you want to please God with your life, you will let love fill you. You will let love flow through you. To everyone. Even those who do not want it. Who will interpret you as being weak because of your love. Even to those who will take advantage of you when you love them. To your enemies.

God does not promise that love will conquer everything *immediately*. But it will conquer everything *eventually*. Love always makes its mark. But sometimes it is a very small mark. Barely noticeable. If you must win now and celebrate the victory today—then you will choose another path to win. Because love rarely works that way. It is a long term, not a quick investment.

Jesus lived a life of love. But he was a "man of sorrows and familiar with suffering."[44] I think he was unbelievably joyful. Yet, deep down in his heart, he was a grieved man. Because most of his love was not returned. And that hurts—as you know. "He came to that which was his own, but his own did not receive him."[45] If you will follow him in living a life of love, you will know deep-seated pain. Maybe a lot of it. But you will never lose your joy. The joy of doing something well. Of having lived and loved well.

People do not know what to do with the love of God. It has to grow on them before they really recognize it for what it is. But the whole process is worth it. The wait and the pain. Because God is always pleased with love. And because love eventually wins.

If you want to finish your life well and stand before our loving Father having really pleased him— then live a life of love. Whatever the cost. Many will ignore your love and even use it against you. But "God is not unjust. He will not forget your work and the love you have shown him as you have helped his people and continue to help them."[46]

Never give up on love. Never switch strategies from love to something else. Why? Because God has promised, love never fails!

Now, we are ready for the challenge. The foundation is set. The rest of the house can be securely built. Since God is love. And since love mattered most to Jesus, to Paul and to every local church. And since

---

44   Isaiah 53:3b
45   John 1:11
46   Hebrews 6:10

love always wins…Let Love Win through YOU!

For Reflection and Discusssion:

What in your life most often defeats you?

44

Let Love Win
Through
YOU!
(Part Four)

"Agape may be aided by seeing, accompanied by feeling, and accomplished by doing, but it is essentially an act of choosing, an act of free will."[47]

"It is characteristic of mature love that it calls into play all man's potentialities; it engages the whole man, so to speak...Acknowledgement of the living God is one path towards love, and the 'yes' of our will to his will unites our intellect, will and sentiments in the all-embracing act of love. But this process is always open-ended; love is never 'finished' and complete; throughout life, it changes and matures and thus remains faithful to itself... The love-story between God and man consists in the very fact that this communion of will increases in a communion of thought and sentiment, and thus our will and God's will increasingly coincide: God's will is no longer an alien will, something imposed on me from without by the commandments, but it is now my own will...."[48]

---

47   Peter Kreeft in *The God Who Loves You*, p 62.

48   Pope Benedict XVI in *The Love of God (Ignatius Press)*, pp 43-44

Chapter 8 – *Let...*

Every Christian develops some theological position regarding God's sovereignty and human responsibility. There are two extremes and many in-betweens. Extreme #1 – God is in control of everything. So we do not need to initiate anything. What he wants to do will get done. We are best to be passive and respond to God's will. Extreme #2 – Man is totally in control of his own destiny and life. He makes it happen. God is passive and responds to our wills. Thankfully, few hold either of these extreme positions.

Most are struggling for some balance in between the extremes. My training would tend more toward the pro-sovereignty side. Which can lead into a passive, wait-and-see-what-God-does strategy.

Both emphases (not the extremes) have clear Scriptural support. God is sovereign and we are responsible agents. He is at work and so are we. At the same time.[49] But two clarifications need to be made so we do not fall into serious error.

In a sinner's regeneration, God works first. Not us. He opens the heart and then we respond.[50] "We love him because he first loved us."[51] We were "dead" in sin and he raised us from spiritual death.[52] We are born again "not of human decision" but "born of God."[53]

---

[49]   See Genesis 50:19-20; Exodus 9:12, 34-35; Psalms 37:4; 115:1-3; Proverbs 8:17; 16:1, 9, 33; Jeremiah 1:5; 18:7-10; John 6:35, 44; Acts 2:22-23; Romans 9:15-16; 10:9-13; 1 Corinthians 4:17; 9:24-27; Ephesians 2:8-10; Philippians 2:12-13; Jude 20-25

[50]   Acts 16:14

[51]   1 John 4:19

[52]   Eph 2:1-5

[53]   John 1:12-13; also 3:3-8

Like the creation of the world, when God says to the darkened human soul, "Let there be light," there is light![54] Our soul's rebirth is, therefore, by his grace not our works.[55]

It is serious when a person denies God as the author or initiator of his salvation. If this error is maintained, he will slip into several serious errors. All which build up his own pride. And cause him to think of himself as being intrinsically better or more worthy than others. This line of thinking is deadly because it sets the man against both God and his Word.[56] It is a lie.

The second clarification needing to be made has direct impact on our understanding of love. Though God initiates our spiritual life, it is wrong to maintain that following our new birth, we must passively wait on God for most things. In the new birth, we are given a new will. A new capacity to desire and to choose. And God wants us, even commands us, to use that will. To freely choose him. It is wrong to be spiritually passive if we have been risen from the dead with new life in Jesus! It is wrong to use our wills to desire and choose anyone other than God. And anything other than love.

This is why I am focusing this chapter on the word, "let." It is something that YOU must do. You must desire and make the choice for the love of God. Because true love is FREE. God wants you who are capable of loving him to love him all the time. With your entire being. He wants you to long for him. To freely come to him. So Scripture invites us, "Come near to God and he will come near to you."[57] Its promises often

---

54   Genesis 1:3; 2 Corinthians 4:6
55   Romans 4:1-7; Ephesians 2:8-9
56   Deuteronomy 7:7-8; Proverbs 3:33-34; 16:18; Matthew 5:3; John 15:1,5,16; James 4:6
57   James 4:8a; also Zechariah 1:3; Mal 3:7

include such words as, "I love those who love me, and those who seek me find me."[58]

God will not compel the Christian to love him. Because true love does not use brute force. As we have seen, love is a thing of peace not pressure. That is one reason why sexual abuse is such a horrible perversion. It is the opposite of true love. Sex crimes are the epitome of self-love. The devil will oppress and force and captivate against your will. He fills a self-enslaved man who murders his "lover" because he cannot endure the thought of her being with another man. Not so the love of God. He will wait until you want him. Until your lesser loves have failed you and you cry out to him. God waits because "love is patient."[59]

When this fact about true love is understood, then we can better understand how God can both "love the world" and yet leave it to itself.[60] A lover naturally desires the beloved to return his love. A true lover will even let the beloved go rather than force love from him. Love always allows for the freedom of the other.

So, what do you want? What and whom will you choose to love? Like the forgiving father of the prodigal son, God is waiting for you to choose him. To come home. To long for him. His promise of love has always said, "You will seek me and find me when you seek me with all your heart."[61]

Many seek God and fall deeply in love with him at the time of their conversion. This is their first love. But, then, they follow others instead of Jesus and let themselves get sidetracked from love. Often to some

---

58   Proverbs 8:17
59   1 Corinthians 13:4
60   John 3:16; Romans 1:24,26,28; Psalms 81:10-12
61   Jeremiah 29:13; also Deuteronomy 4:29; Psalm 119:58; Isaiah 45:19,22

good thing. But not the first thing. The best thing. Let love back in. Back on top. And you will find both an amazing response from God and renewed power in your life. Love will begin to win through you when you desire it to be first.

For Reflection and Discussion:

How often do you exercise your freedom of choice to let God's love flow through you?

What hinders this from happening more often?

"Love is indeed 'ecstasy' not in the sense of a moment of intoxication, but rather as a journey, an ongoing exodus out of the closed inward-looking self towards its liberation through self-giving, and thus towards authentic self-discovery and indeed the discovery of God: 'Whoever seeks to gain his life will lose it, but whoever loses his life will preserve it' (Lk 17:33), as Jesus says throughout the Gospels…. Starting from the depths of his own sacrifice and of the love that reaches fulfillment therein, he also portrays in these words the essence of love and indeed of human life itself."[62]

"Fundamental to the experience of perfect love is the loss of self-concern. It is to stop worrying about how useful things may be to us, and instead to pay attention to them as separate centers of reality. Usually we are aware only of ourselves as centers of reality and forget that each of us is but one reality among billions and billions of others. We experience others not as centers of value in themselves, but as beings in orbit around ourselves."[63]

62   Pope Benedict XVI in *God is Love*, p 22
63   Diogenes Allen in *Love (Cowley Publications)*, p 10.

Chapter 9 – Let **Love...**

Since "God is love," all types of love reflect him. Either a little or a lot. But even love can become an idol when we allow a lesser love to take the supreme place of the love of God in our hearts. When we take one of the reflections to be the real thing. To become true love to us. Human friendship, romantic love, brotherly love, marital union, fondness, kindness, compassion, are all lesser loves. These are good and enrich our lives. Unless they demand the elimination of God's love from its place of top priority.

Some other lesser loves are far dimmer reflections of God's love than these are. Love of money. Love of control. Passionate love without thought of consequences. Love for pets more than love for humans. Love of things. Things we collect and cherish. The things we get really upset about when they get broken or scratched. Or misplaced. Or touched by a child! When any of these loves replace God's love, one thing inevitably begins to happen. We begin to lose instead of winning. When our lesser loves fail to deliver the lasting euphoria we expected and wanted, we tend to get angry and impatient. Things can go south rather quickly, leading even to pessimism, depression and hopelessness.

Lesser loves eventually lose their fun and the satisfaction they bring us. We live in a world filled with anger, anxiety, depression and sadness because the joy brought by our lesser loves never lasts long enough. Only God's love never fails.

The whole world's experience proves that *we do not know what God's love is without his help*. Without him showing us and explaining it to us. Because we make our lesser loves out to be true love. Which they aren't. "**This is how we know what love is**: Jesus Christ laid down his life for us."[64] Jesus shows us the great love of God. Not only in his supreme act of dying for us. But in everything he did. And one big reason he was hated and killed was that he exposed the lesser loves of those around him. Loves which they did not want to give up. His love even for his enemies led him to honestly reveal their self-centered loves. That is what love does. It helps others by showing them that their supreme love in life will fail them. And they did not like that. Anymore than we do today. Make no mistake about it. You and I do not know what true, agape love is until God enlightens us.

We can put it this way: no one knows true love apart from the Spirit of God. "God has poured out his love into our hearts by the Holy Spirit, whom he has given us."[65] What we know naturally and indelibly is self-love. We are drawn to that which attracts us. Or adds something to us. We rarely love someone or something for very long if they cease to benefit our lives.

God's love is different. "But God demonstrates his own love for us in this: While we were still sinners, Christ died for us."[66] He loved us while we were running from him. Not towards him. We were angry rebels not admiring followers. We naturally hate his selfless love because we are consumers. Not givers. We love that which adds to or benefits us. God loves ugly-hearted, mean-spirited, holier-than-thou humans. He loves what we cannot love because we love only what in some way helps us. He loves us as we are because it is simply his eternal nature to so love humankind.

---

64   1 John 3:16a
65   Romans 5:5b
66   Romans 5:8

We can't let love win through us until we recognize what true love is. God's love is selfless. It is a love that ever flows outward. Agape love always seeks the good of the beloved. Love always leads one to cherish the other more than the self. As Paul said, love "is not self-seeking."[67] Unlike ours, God's love is not self-focused. We quickly grow miserable because we are self-absorbed. Deep down our favorite love song has one chorus, "Gimme, gimme, gimme." No matter how each stanza may extol another, the chorus inevitably returns us to our bottom line. It's about Me.

One of the great tests of whether the love within us is from God or not is if we embrace what Jesus said to all his followers: "You have heard that it was said, 'Love your neighbor and hate your enemy.' But I tell you: Love your enemies and pray for those who persecute you."[68] Wow! Cherishing one's opponents. Praying for their good instead of responding to them in anger or hatred. That love would certainly challenge and change the world. Maybe not immediately. But inevitably. That love wins! Just read the book of Acts. Or listen to the inspired standard Paul passed on to Christians living in Rome. In the city ruled over by Caesar Nero.

"Love must be sincere...Bless those who persecute you; bless and do not curse...Do not repay anyone evil for evil... If it is possible, as far as it depends on you, live at peace with everyone. Do not take revenge, my friends...Do not be overcome by evil, but overcome evil with good."[69]

None of us can love that way without God's help. But the Roman Christians did. And we can, too. If we let his

---

67   1 Corinthians 13:3b

68   Matthew 5:43-44

69   Romans 12:9, 14, 17-19, 21

love fill us. All you need do is desire and determine, by his grace, to "keep yourselves in God's love."[70]

For all of you who have put your heart out there only to have it crushed. The abused. The unappreciated, forsaken and overlooked. For those who have given up on love. And withdrawn into your own isolated, lonely, unfulfilled life. The only safe place you know. This love cannot fail you because it is God's love. You have tried lesser loves and have been burned. It is time to trust in God's unfailing love. To experience what David enjoyed, in the midst of all his trials, "I am like an olive tree flourishing in the house of God; I trust in God's unfailing love forever and ever."[71]

Will the Lord love you? In a way far better than your lesser loves ever could. He will both love you and begin to fill you with the love that looks like this: A love that is patient. That is not proud, rude or easily angered. A love that keeps no record of wrongs and always trusts the heart of the beloved. A love full of hope.[72]

Ask God to replace your most cherished loves with his great love. Give your mind over to the love that all lesser loves imperfectly reflect and fall far short of. Let your emotions, speech and actions be empowered by one principle: The love of Jesus. Let love win through you!

---

70   Jude 21
71   Psalm 52:8
72   1 Corinthians 13:4-7

For Reflection and Discussion:

Do you know anyone who seems to be perpetually filled with God's Love?

What makes him/her different than most others?

"Goodness and love are as real as their opposites, and, in truth, far more real, though I say this mindful of the enormous evils like Nazi Germany. But love is the final   reality; and anyone who does not understand this, be he writer or sage, is a man flawed in his wisdom."[73]

"In this world, despite all the pleasure and healing it   brings, Christian love will always be a matter of loving in hard places. But none of it as hard as what God did: "God   demonstrates his own love for us in this: While we were still sinners, Christ died for us(Rom 5:8)… One day the hard places will be gone. But the love will remain, unalloyed, immensely rich, reflecting in small and glorious ways the immeasurable love we have received."[74]

73   Sheldon Vanauken in *A Divine Mercy(HarperCollins Publishers)* , p 164.
74   DA Carson in *Love in Hard Places*, p195.

Chapter 10 – Let Love *Win...*

What makes love such a winner? God makes love a winner. Scripture has concluded that since God is love—and God will win—then love must in fact win. But we have seen that love's winning does NOT mean always immediately. In fact, since our hearts are wrapped so tightly in false loves, it usually takes time to unwrap them. Like peeling an onion. And often we cry when the false loves are getting peeled away. The process often hurts. Both us and others. But it is worth the effort.

When love wins, everything good wins. Another way to say it is that love is like oil in a car's engine. It makes every part run better. Without it, every part will wear out and eventually stop functioning. But with love, every part that is needed operates smoothly and efficiently. Like adding oil, adding God's love fixes problems. It wins.

Paul prayed that the Ephesians would be "rooted and established in love"[75] Love is the foundation. The root. Good things will grow from the root of love. Paul wrote that love helps all other Christian virtues.

"Therefore, as God's chosen people, holy and dearly loved, clothe yourselves with compassion, kindness, humility, gentleness and patience. Bear with each other and forgive whatever grievances you may have against one another. Forgive as the Lord forgave you. And over all these virtues put on love, which binds them all together in perfect unity."[76]

I hope you really got what he said about love. It binds all other virtues together in perfect unity. It brings

---

75   Ephesians 3:17
76   Colossians 3:12-14

them all into sync. The KJV put it this way, "And above all these things put on charity, which is the bond of perfectness." Jesus taught that love, alone, would help Christians live in completeness and maturity.[77] Paul taught that love would lead the Christian to "be filled to the measure of all the fullness of God."[78]

Let's see how this works. How love actually leads the Christian to win in regard to every area of personal struggle. When this truth grabs you, your life will change! Put simply – every problem at its root is a love problem.

Your heart is convicted of your not praying enough. Your problem is not mainly a prayer problem. It is a love problem. So, don't pray that God would help you to pray. Pray that God will fill you with love. When you love God, you will want to communicate with God. Because love must communicate with the beloved one! Try to keep two people in love from communicating. When the love of Jesus fills you, you will desire to communicate with the Father. Love is the solution to a prayer problem.

Let's say you struggle with unholiness. Who doesn't in some way? There is some sin that keeps tripping you up. Many would counsel that you need to ask for self discipline. Or for awareness. Or for hatred of sin. The ability to die to sin. These are true enough. But I would first suggest that unholiness is chiefly a love problem. If you want to be holy, ask God to fill you with his love. How does love win in regard to sin? Because love will set you apart for the beloved. And that is the definition of holy – to be set apart for God.

Adultery is much more of a temptation when

---

77   Matthew 5:43-48
78   Ephesians 3:19

the marriage is on the rocks than when the couple is consumed by true love for one another. Love leads to holiness. To separation from sin and temptation. Love makes you want to remain pure and faithful to the one you love. Love is the foundation of holiness.

Perhaps you really lack courage to witness of Christ to others. Maybe to certain people at work. Or to Jewish people. Or Muslims. So what should you do? Pray for courage? Not primarily. Pray for the love of God to fill you. You will love those whom God loves when you are filled with his love. And "God so loved the world..."[79] There is no one in the world whom you will not learn to love when your heart is filled with the love of Christ. Do you think I would need courage to protect my wife if she were threatened? Of course not! My love for her breathes courage. However big or armed or many would try to hurt her, I would try my best to protect her. Even to death. Love for another creates courage.

Do you struggle with pride? I would lead you to pray for love before asking for humility. Because "love is not proud."[80] Love ever denies itself and seeks the good of the other. Love is the root of humility. We think little about ourselves when we are thinking of others. And that is precisely what love does.

So whatever it is: anger, forcefulness, disobedience, impatience, lust, laziness, drugs, etc. Love is the solution. This is likely why you have struggled so long against a certain sin. Your victory lies in your loving Jesus more than you have been loving yourself and your sin. A greater love can break the power of a lesser love. When one loves God with all his heart, he

---

79   John 3:16
80   1 Corinthians 13:4

will have a power over the pain that has often driven him to drink. The love of Christ is far more powerful than the numbing power of one's drug of choice. Love is much more effective than any other weapon in our fight with sin.

Perhaps the chief reason so many Christians struggle so long with addictions is that they have never had the Spirit replace love for the substance by the love of Jesus. They go away to rehabs and try to get stronger in a number of ways. But too few who turn to the noble-but-lesser loves like, being a good husband, supporting a family, holding down a job, being a good role model, strengthening society, etc. remain drug-free. These lesser loves do not always supply the impetus needed to say NO when tempted. Because the power of drugs, especially crack cocaine, is phenomenal. But the love of Christ controlling one's being will always win against a lesser love. That love never fails unless we give up on it and turn to a lesser love.

I hope this encourages you. Just think! Love can win much more quickly than any other remedy. You may have struggled long because you have been turning to the wrong spiritual medicine. When you take a good strong dose of the love of Christ, every idol is dashed. And its power over you will be weakened as long as you choose to remain in God's love. Listen carefully to Jesus: "As the Father has loved me, so have I loved you. Now remain in my love."[81] As long as you rest in his love, you will make amazing progress.

Paul put it this way, "Be imitators of God, therefore, as dearly loved children and live a life of love, just as Christ loved us and gave himself up for

---

81   John 15:9

us as a fragrant offering and sacrifice to God."[82] Love is not just an option. It is a way of life. We must live in love. Not just turn to it briefly. We need a lifestyle of love. And it usually takes a bit of time to develop a new lifestyle. But it doesn't have to take long. God "is able to do immeasurably more than all we ask or imagine, according to his power that is at work within us."[83] Let love WIN through you!

For Reflection and Discussion:

What sin most often wins in your life?

How can you beat it?

---

82   Ephesians 5:1-2
83   Ephesians 3:20

*"To love one's neighbor means…
essentially to will to exist equally for
every human being without exception."*[84]

84   Soren Kierkegaard in *Works of Love*, p 92.

Chapter 11 – Let love win **through...**

The love I have been speaking about is a personal attribute. It is not a characteristic of pets or trees. Of squirrels or chimps. It is the gift of God for those who bear his image.[85] I know you want to believe that your pet loves you. It might have some affection for you – but that is not to be confused with the love of God. Do something to the pet that makes you its enemy and see how long the affection continues. But Jesus told us as Christians that we are to love our enemies. We need not strike back at them.

Christians must realize that we are the Body of Christ. We represent him on earth. What is done to us, he views as done to himself.[86] The good that he would do on earth is to be done chiefly through us. So we pray, "Your will be done on earth as it is in heaven."[87] We should love and serve God as the angels in heaven wait on him to do his bidding.[88] We should not wait for the next person to do it.

In teaching us who is our neighbor, whom we are to love, Jesus gave the parable of the Good Samaritan. Read the story again and note the final words of Jesus to you.

"On one occasion an expert in the law stood up to test Jesus. 'Teacher,' he asked, 'what must I do to inherit eternal life?' 'What is written in the Law?' he replied. 'How do you read it?' He answered: 'Love the Lord your God with all your heart and with all your soul and

---

85   Genesis 1:26-28
86   Matthew 25:40; Acts 9:4; Hebrews 6:10
87   Matthew 6:10b
88   Psalm 103:20-21; Hebrews 1:14

with all your strength and with all your mind;'
and, 'Love your neighbor as yourself.' 'You have
answered correctly,' Jesus replied. 'Do this and
you will live.' But he wanted to justify himself,
so he asked Jesus, 'And who is my neighbor?'"

"In reply Jesus said: 'A man was going
down from Jerusalem to Jericho, when he fell
into the hands of robbers. They stripped him of
his clothes, beat him and went away, leaving
him half dead. A priest happened to be going
down the same road, and when he saw the man,
he passed by on the other side. So too, a Levite,
when he came to the place and saw him, passed
by on the other side. But a Samaritan, as he
traveled, came where the man was; and when
he saw him, he took pity on him. He went to him
and bandaged his wounds, pouring on oil and
wine. Then he put the man on his own donkey,
took him to an inn and took care of him. The
next day he took out two silver coins[c] and gave
them to the innkeeper. 'Look after him,' he said,
'and when I return, I will reimburse you for any
extra expense you may have.'"

"'Which of these three do you think was a
neighbor to the man who fell into the hands of
robbers?' The expert in the law replied, 'The one
who had mercy on him.' Jesus told him, 'Go and
do likewise.'"[89]

Let love win **through** you. Not through
someone else. Not through the church or the
pastor. Not through the Federal, State or City
Governments. Not through Bill Gates or Oprah
Winfrey. Not through the Salvation Army or

---

89   Luke 10:25-37

World Vision. Let love win through you! Step up. Just show up. Get out and get involved. With people and their needs. Let love win through you today.

For Reflection and Discussion:

What can you do TODAY from true love?

"I suspect that one of the reasons why there are so many exhortations in the New Testament for Christians to love other Christians is because this is not an easy thing to do."[90]

"The love Jesus bore for outcasts and sinners was not only the love of God incarnated in his person but also his own love as a human being. The uncaused, spontaneous agape he bore for sinners was a love he manifested not merely because he was God but also because he was truly human— freely and sinlessly man, the perfect embodiment of all God meant and means humanity to be. It is precisely here, in the true Adam, that we see human nature for the very first time as God intended it to be...."[91]

---

90   DA Carson in *Love in Hard Places*, pp 60-61.
91   Alan Torrance in *Nothing Greater Nothing Better*, pp 133-34.

Chapter 12 – Let love win through **YOU!**

Don't sell yourself short. Though we are sinners, we are not worthless. In fact, your worth to God can be somewhat measured by the price he was willing to pay to redeem you. He gave his Son for you. You are not trash to God. The prodigal son, when returning to his father, said, "I am no longer worthy to be called your son…" Did the father agree? No, he said to his servants, "Quick! Bring the best robe and put it on him. Put a ring on his finger and sandals on his feet. Bring the fattened calf and kill it. Let's have a feast and celebrate. For this son of mine was dead and is alive again; he was lost and is found. So they began to celebrate!"[92] Let love win through YOU.

Sure you have messed up. We all have. But do you really think that disqualifies you? That it somehow turns God's heart of love away from you? Remember the gospel. Jesus lived the life of pure love that heaven demands of us all. And he died for all our sins. Nothing was left undone for us. Only believe.[93]

As a result of this Good News, the apostle Paul rejoiced:

"Who shall separate us from the love of Christ? Shall trouble or hardships or persecution or famine or nakedness or danger or sword?... No, in all these things we are more than conquerors through him who loved us. For I am convinced that neither death nor life, neither angels nor demons, neither present nor the future, nor any powers, neither height nor depth, nor anything else in all creation, will be able to separate

---

92   Luke 15:21b-24
93   Mark 9:23-24; Luke 8:50; John 1:12; 6:28-29; 20:27; Acts
       16:31; Romans 3:21-23; Hebrews 11:6

us from the love of God that is in Christ Jesus our Lord."[94]

God has been all over your life. And with you. "For from him and through him and to him are all things."[95] Through all your failures and advances. They have served God's purposes. One of which is that they make you absolutely unique. Struggles with sin show that you are real. That you know what it is to be drawn in by the world. To open your heart to it. You know what it feels like to have had your dreams dashed by trusting in sin's deceptions. By making a lesser love your god. Those experiences allow your individual story to glorify the best love, the grace of God.

Our failures also rightly humble us. They make us useful to the Lord because he "opposes the proud but gives grace to the humble."[96] Don't let your past or your present limit your future! Become great for God today. You know how much he has loved you. How much he has freely forgiven you. Turn this to your profit. Let it become your greatest asset, just like the sinful woman who lavishly anointed him. Of her Jesus said, "Therefore I tell you, her many sins have been forgiven –for she loved much. But he who has been forgiven little loves little."[97]

God desires to use you mightily. But, as we have seen, he will not force himself on you. He wants the main part of your being. Your heart. The place where your love resides. That's all. He wants you to come home. So he can fill you with his love. And by it—with his power.

As we close this book, I hope you will never forget

94   Romans 8:35-39
95   Romans 11:36a
96   James 4:6
97   Luke 7:47

its message. Love should guide your every thought, word and deed. Share this message with others. Help them on to the victory that Jesus wants us all to experience NOW! You can help stop the selfishness that strangles God's love from flowing through others. You can become an agent of loving change for your small group, church, your denomination. But be patient in prayer, realizing that your loving God is in control. He will make it happen.

Today's lack of love is why so few Christians radiate much evidence of the indwelling Holy Spirit. This is how he who is called "the power of the Highest"[98] can reside within us without mightily empowering us. A loveless heart grieves and shuts down the mighty work of the Spirit of Love in and through us. He is there, waiting for you to deal with this one great sin. To repent of your thoughts, feelings, words and deeds that are devoid of the love of Christ. Repent and return to your first love and watch the door for great progress open. Turn away from every lesser love and let the love of Christ compel you.[99] Then just "keep in step with the Spirit"[100] of love. Make every moment a moment of love. Every person an object of God's love pouring through you. And simply continue to live that life of love more and more as he enables you.[101]

There is one final passage I want to leave with you. It is a special message from God to YOU. It is for all those who choose to be filled with his love. Memorize it and expect its every promise to be yours. It is a promise that God's love will win through you—if you open your life to it.

---

98   Luke 1:35
99   2 Corinthians 5:14a
100   Galatians 5:25
101   1 Thessalonians 4:9-10

*"**Because he loves me**," says the LORD, "I will **rescue** him; I will **protect** him, for he acknowledges my name. He will call upon me, and I will **answer** him; I will be **with him in trouble**, I will **deliver** him and **honor** him. With long life will I **satisfy** him and **show him my salvation**."*[102]

For Reflection or Discussion:

What works of love should NOW flow from your life as proof of your repentance?

After a few days of letting love win through you, what is the "circle of influence" (the people closest and most involved in your life) given to you by God with whom you could share the message of the love of Christ?

---

102   Psalm 91:14-16

Other Works By Dr. Ed Gross:

Charles Hodge's <u>Systematic Theology</u>, abridged, with study questions. Phillipsburg, NJ: P & R Publishing, 1988, 1997.

<u>Miracles, Demons & Spiritual Warfare</u>: An Urgent Call for Discernment. Grand Rapids, MI: Baker Book House, 1990.

<u>Christianity Without A King</u>: The Results of Abandoning Christ's Lordship. Columbus, GA: Brentwood Press, 1992.

<u>Will My Children Go To Heaven</u>? Hope and Help for Believing Parents. Phillipsburg, NJ: P&R Pubishing, 1995.

Several articles in <u>Evangelical Dictionary of World Missions</u>, edited by A Scott Moreau. Grand Rapids, MI: Baker Book House, 2000.

Ed Gross serves as the Coordinator of Strategic Alliances with CityNet Ministries in Philadelphia, PA and teaches at Back to the Bible Training College in Barberton, South Africa.

www.citynetphilly.org
www.bbtc.co.za

To follow his ministry & blog, visit Ed's website at:
www.edwardngross.com

Made in the USA
Lexington, KY
04 August 2010